Copyright © 2025 by David Twain

All rights reserved. No part of this book may be reproduced, stored in a retrieval system, or transmitted in any form or by any means, electronic, mechanical, photocopying, recording, or otherwise, without prior written permission by the author.

This book keeps things simple and focuses only on Google Drive, giving you clear, easy-to-follow information to help you understand it better.

Whether you're brand new to technology or already have some experience, this book is here to help. My goal is to make you feel confident, inspire your creativity, and show you that learning Google Drive can be easy and enjoyable.

Table of Contents

Introduction

1. What is Google Drive?

Overview of Cloud Storage

Cloud storage is a service that allows users to store data, such as files and documents, on remote servers that can be accessed through the internet. Instead of saving files on a physical device, cloud storage lets you save them securely in a virtual space. This enables users to access their data from multiple devices, like a smartphone, tablet, or computer, without the need for physical storage devices like USB drives or external hard drives.

Google Drive is one of the most popular cloud storage services, offered by Google. With Google Drive, you can upload, store, and share files such as documents, photos, videos, and more. All files stored on Google Drive are synced across your devices, allowing you to access them anytime, anywhere, as long as you have an internet connection.

Why Google Drive is Essential for Beginners

Google Drive is particularly useful for beginners due to its simplicity, wide accessibility, and integration with other Google services. As a beginner, you can start using Google Drive with little technical knowledge, and it provides a seamless experience for managing and organizing your files. It's an all-in-one solution that lets you store files, collaborate with others, and access your data without worrying about storage limits or complex systems.

For those already using Gmail or other Google services, Google Drive is a natural extension, providing easy access and synchronization across these platforms. Additionally, it comes with a generous amount of free storage, making it ideal for individuals who don't want to worry about purchasing expensive external storage devices.

Key Benefits of Using Google Drive

1. **Free Storage:** Google Drive offers 15GB of free storage to all users, which is more than enough for most beginners to get started with storing and organizing files.

2. **Ease of Use:** The interface is user-friendly and intuitive, with drag-and-drop functionality, making it easy to upload and organize files.
3. **Accessibility:** Google Drive can be accessed from any device with an internet connection, allowing you to work from anywhere, whether you're using a computer, tablet, or smartphone.
4. **Collaboration:** Google Drive allows multiple people to collaborate on the same document in real time. Whether you're working on a Google Doc, Sheet, or Slide, you can edit and make changes together with others, and see them immediately.
5. **Security and Backup:** Google Drive automatically backs up your files and data. It also offers advanced security features like two-factor authentication to keep your files safe.
6. **Integration with Google Services:** Google Drive integrates with other Google products such as Gmail, Google Docs, Google Sheets, and Google Slides, making it easier to manage files in a comprehensive ecosystem.

How Google Drive Differs from Other Cloud Storage Services

While there are many cloud storage services available today, Google Drive offers several features that set it apart from the competition:

*   **Generous Free Storage:** Many cloud storage services, such as Dropbox or iCloud, offer less free storage space than Google Drive. The 15GB of free storage on Google Drive can store a considerable number of files, images, and documents before needing to upgrade.

- **Seamless Google Ecosystem Integration:** Google Drive works flawlessly with other Google services like Gmail, Google Docs, Google Sheets, and Google Calendar. This tight integration makes it easy to create, store, and share documents without needing separate tools.
- **Collaborative Features:** Google Drive's collaboration tools are second to none. You can share files and folders with others, assign permissions, and edit files together in real time. While other cloud services also offer collaboration, Google's suite of productivity tools makes this process incredibly efficient.
- **Offline Access:** Google Drive allows you to work on files offline with the Google Drive app on your desktop or mobile device. This makes it easier to access your files even when you're not connected to the internet.

2. How to Get Started with Google Drive

Creating a Google Account

To use Google Drive, you need a Google Account. If you already have a Gmail account, you can use the same login credentials to access Google Drive. If you don't have a Google Account yet, here's how to create one:

1. **Go to the Google Account Creation Page:** Open a web browser and go to https://accounts.google.com/signup.

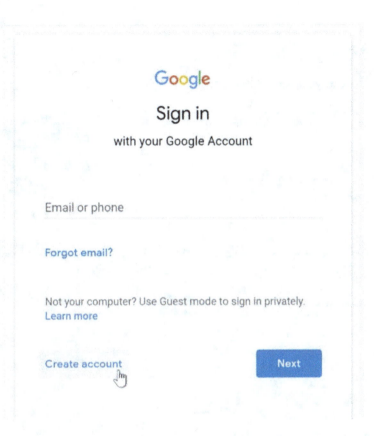

Google

Sign in

with your Google Account

Email or phone

Forgot email?

Not your computer? Use Guest mode to sign in privately.
Learn more

Create account

Next

2. **Fill in Your Details:** You'll need to provide your first and last name, create a unique username (this will become your Gmail address), and create a password. Make sure your password is strong and easy to remember.

Google

Create your Google Account

First name

Last name

Username   @gmail.com

You can use letters, numbers & periods

Use my current email address instead

Password   Confirm

Use 8 or more characters with a mix of letters, numbers & symbols

One account. All of Google working for you.

Sign in instead   Next

Create your Google Account

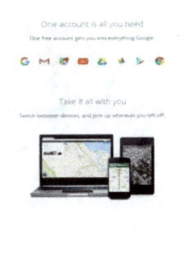

3. **Verify Your Account:** Google will ask you to verify your identity by providing a phone number for account recovery and security purposes. This helps you regain access to your account in case you forget your password or if there is suspicious activity.

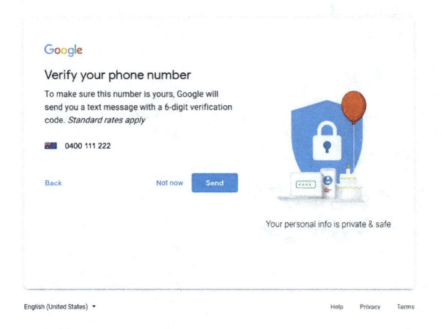

Google

Verify your phone number

To make sure this number is yours, Google will send you a text message with a 6-digit verification code. *Standard rates apply*

0400 111 222

Back   Not now   Send

Your personal info is private & safe

English (United States) ▾   Help   Privacy   Terms

4. **Agree to the Terms of Service:** Once you've filled out the information, review Google's terms of service and privacy policy, and then click "I agree" to proceed.

5. **Set Up Your Profile:** After account creation, you can add a profile picture (optional) and adjust your privacy settings. Once your Google Account is set up, you can access Google Drive.

Once you have a Google Account, you're ready to start using Google Drive. If you already have a Gmail account, simply log in and proceed with the next steps.

Setting Up Google Drive on Desktop, Mobile, and Web

Google Drive can be accessed on any device with an internet connection, including desktops, laptops, tablets, and smartphones. Here's how to set it up across different platforms:

1. **On Desktop (Web):**
   o **Access via Browser:** On your computer, open your preferred web browser (Google Chrome is recommended but any browser will work). Go to https://drive.google.com.
   o **Sign in:** Log in to your Google Account using the username and password you created.
   o **Start Using Google Drive:** Once logged in, you'll be taken to the Google Drive dashboard where you can start uploading files, creating folders, and organizing your content.
2. **On Mobile Devices (iOS and Android):**
   o **Download the App:** To access Google Drive on your mobile device, download the Google Drive app from the App Store (for iOS) or Google Play Store (for Android).
   o **Sign in:** Once the app is installed, open it and log in with your Google Account credentials.
   o **Using the App:** You can now upload, organize, and manage your files directly from your phone or tablet. Google Drive also allows you to access your files offline, making it easy to stay productive even when you're not connected to the internet.
3. **Syncing Across Devices:**

- ○ **Automatic Syncing:** Any file you upload or change on Google Drive via one device will automatically sync across all devices connected to the same Google Account. For example, if you upload a document from your desktop, you can access it from your phone without needing to do anything else.
- ○ **Google Backup and Sync (Optional):** If you prefer a desktop client for syncing files between your computer and Google Drive, you can download and install the "Backup and Sync" app, which will automatically sync selected folders from your computer to Google Drive.

Chapter 1: Getting to Know Google Drive

1. Navigating the Google Drive Interface

Web Interface Overview

The Google Drive web interface is where most users will interact with their files, organize them, and manage their settings. Here's what you'll find when you access Google Drive on your browser:

1. **Navigation Bar**: At the top of the screen, you'll see the main navigation bar, which contains links to different parts of Google Drive, including:
   - **My Drive**: This is where all your personal files and folders are stored.
   - **Shared Drives**: These are drives shared with you by others, useful for group projects or work teams.
   - **Computers**: If you've set up Google Drive to sync files from specific computers, you'll find these here.
   - **Trash**: Files and folders you've deleted are temporarily placed in Trash and can be restored if needed.
2. **Search Bar**: Directly below the navigation bar, you'll find the search bar. This allows you to quickly find files by typing keywords, file names, or using filters (like type of file, owner, or date modified).
3. **File Preview Area**: When you select a file, the preview area shows a quick view of that file's content. You can preview

most file types directly from Google Drive, such as PDFs, images, documents, and videos.

Understanding the Sidebar, File View, and Settings Menu

1. **Sidebar Overview**: The sidebar, typically found on the left side of the screen, gives you quick access to important areas of Google Drive:
   - **Quick Access**: Shows frequently accessed files, recent files, and suggestions based on your usage.
   - **My Drive**: Displays all of your personal files and folders. You can organize, upload, and create new files here.
   - **Shared with Me**: Displays files and folders shared with you by others.
   - **Recent**: A quick way to view the most recently modified or accessed files.
   - **Starred**: Files you've starred for easy access will appear here.
   - **Trash**: Deleted items reside here for easy recovery or permanent deletion.

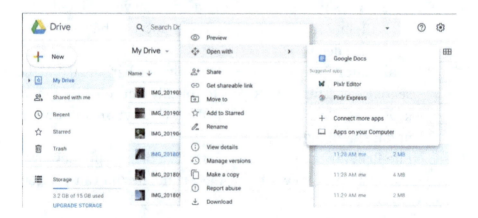

2. **File View**: The main area in the center of the screen displays your files in either a grid or list view. In grid view, file icons are displayed as thumbnails, while in list view, files are shown in a detailed list with names, types, and modification dates.

   o **Grid View**: Ideal for visual files, such as images, videos, or presentations, allowing you to see thumbnails.

   o **List View**: Best for documents or files that don't need visual representation. It gives you more information at a glance, such as the file's size and when it was last modified.

3. **Settings Menu**: To access Google Drive's settings, click on the gear icon in the top-right corner of the screen. Here you can adjust various preferences, such as:

   o **General Settings**: Language preferences, default file format settings, and viewing options.

   o **Notifications**: Control when and how you receive notifications about file activities, such as shared items, comments, and updates.

- o **Offline Mode**: Turn on offline access to files, allowing you to view and edit them even when you don't have an internet connection.
- o **Manage Apps**: View and manage third-party apps that are connected to Google Drive, such as PDF editors or image converters.

Customizing Your Google Drive Layout

Google Drive offers several ways to personalize the layout of your files and folders to improve your workflow and access:

1. **Changing Views**:
   - o **Grid or List View**: Choose whether you want files to be displayed as icons (grid view) or as a list with detailed information (list view). You can toggle between the two modes based on your preference for visual or organized layouts.
2. **Sorting Options**: You can sort files in ascending or descending order based on:
   - o **Name**
   - o **Last Modified**
   - o **Last Opened**
   - o **File Size** Sorting helps you find specific files quickly, especially when your Google Drive becomes cluttered.
3. **Color Coding Folders**: Right-click on any folder in Google Drive to change its color. This is a useful way to visually organize your folders, making it easier to locate important ones at a glance.

4. **Starring Files and Folders**: To quickly access important files, you can "star" them. Right-click on a file and choose "Add star" to mark it. Starred items will appear in the "Starred" section in the sidebar for easy access.

2. Google Drive Mobile App Overview

Installing Google Drive on iOS and Android

1. **For iOS (iPhone/iPad)**:
   o Open the **App Store** on your iOS device.
   o In the search bar, type **Google Drive**.
   o Tap on the **Google Drive app** and then press **Install**.
   o Once the app is installed, tap **Open** to launch it.
   o Sign in with your **Google Account** credentials to start using the app.
2. **For Android**:
   o Open the **Google Play Store** on your Android device.
   o In the search bar, type **Google Drive**.
   o Tap the **Google Drive app** and then press **Install**.
   o Once installed, tap **Open** to launch the app.
   o Log in using your **Google Account** to start managing your files on Google Drive.

App Interface and Basic Navigation

The Google Drive mobile app interface is designed to provide similar functionality to the web version, but optimized for touchscreens. Here's a breakdown of the key features:

1. **Home Screen**:

- The home screen displays your most recent files and folders, with quick access to the **My Drive**, **Shared with Me**, **Starred**, and **Trash** sections. You can also see any file suggestions or recent activity.

2. **Navigation Menu**:
   - **Menu Icon (three horizontal lines)**: Tap this icon in the upper-left corner to open the navigation menu. From here, you can quickly access your files, shared items, starred files, and settings.
   - **Search Bar**: At the top, there's a search bar for quickly finding files, much like the web interface.

3. **Main File Area**:
   - This area displays your files, which you can tap to open, share, or edit. Tap and hold a file for more options, such as moving it, deleting it, or starring it.

4. **Floating Action Button**:
   - The **+** button at the bottom-right corner allows you to upload new files, create new folders, or create new Google Docs, Sheets, Slides, or Forms directly from the app.

5. **Settings**:
   - You can access app settings by tapping on the **gear icon** in the menu. Here you can adjust your preferences, manage notifications, and enable or disable offline mode.

6. **Offline Mode**:
   - You can mark specific files for offline access by tapping on a file, then selecting the three-dot menu icon. Choose "Available offline" to ensure the file is accessible even when you don't have an internet connection.

Chapter 2: Storing and Organizing Files in Google Drive

1. Uploading Files and Folders

Uploading from Desktop, Mobile, and Web

Uploading files and folders to Google Drive is a simple and essential task for storing your documents, images, videos, and more. Here's how to upload across different platforms:

1. **From Desktop (Web Version)**:
    - o **Step 1**: Open your browser and navigate to **drive.google.com**.
    - o **Step 2**: In the Google Drive interface, click the **+ New** button on the left-hand side.

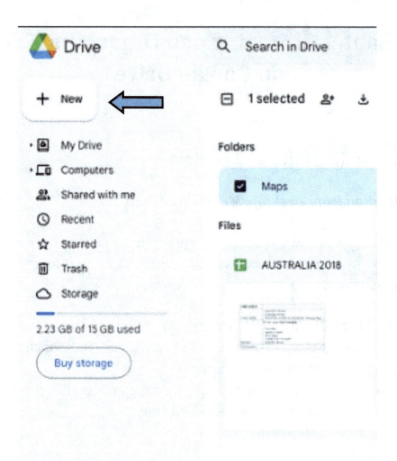

- ○ **Step 3**: You will see two options:
  - ▪ **File Upload**: Choose this to upload individual files from your computer. Browse your device, select the file, and click **Open** to begin uploading.
  - ▪ **Folder Upload**: Choose this to upload an entire folder. Browse for the folder, select it, and click **Upload**.

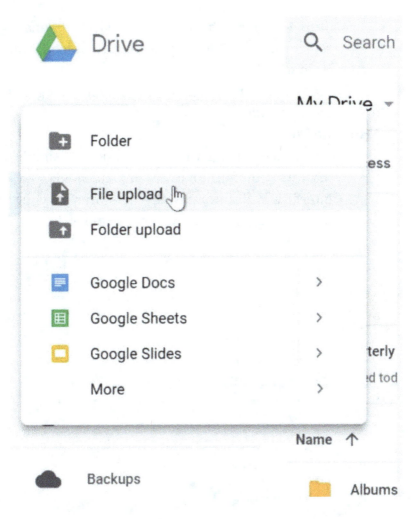

- ○ **Step 4**: Once the upload begins, you'll see the file(s) or folder appear in your "My Drive" section.
2. **From Mobile (iOS/Android)**:
   - ○ **Step 1**: Open the **Google Drive app** on your device.
   - ○ **Step 2**: Tap the **+** icon in the bottom-right corner of the screen.
   - ○ **Step 3**: Select **Upload** to choose files or folders from your phone or tablet.

- o **Step 4**: Browse through your device's file manager, select the files/folders you want to upload, and tap **Upload** to begin.
  - o **Step 5**: The files will appear in your Google Drive once uploaded.
3. **From the Web**:
  - o The process from the web version is simple and intuitive. All files that are uploaded via the web interface will automatically be stored in your "My Drive" unless moved to a specific folder.

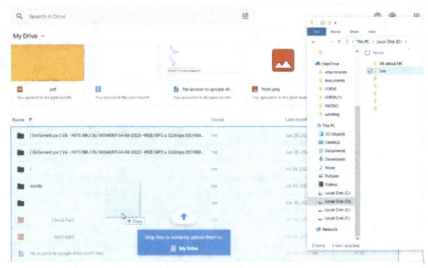

Drag and Drop Files from PC to Google Drive

Supported File Types

Google Drive supports a wide range of file types, making it an all-in-one storage solution for various media, documents, and more. Here's a breakdown of common file types supported:

- **Documents**: PDF, DOCX, TXT, ODT, HTML
- **Spreadsheets**: XLSX, CSV, ODS
- **Presentations**: PPTX, ODP
- **Images**: JPG, PNG, GIF, BMP, TIFF
- **Audio**: MP3, WAV, AAC
- **Video**: MP4, MOV, AVI, MKV, WMV
- **Other**: ZIP files, EPUB, etc.

You can upload almost any file type to Google Drive, and it will be stored as is. For certain file types like documents, you can also use Google Docs, Sheets, and Slides to edit directly within the platform.

Managing Large File Uploads

Uploading large files (such as high-definition videos, large presentations, or large datasets) can sometimes take longer and may need special consideration:

- **Upload Speed**: Make sure you have a stable and fast internet connection to avoid interruptions. If the upload is interrupted, Google Drive will resume from where it left off, so you don't lose progress.
- **Use Google Drive's Desktop App**: The **Google Drive for Desktop** app allows you to sync files automatically from your computer. This method is more efficient for large files, as it handles uploads in the background without requiring you to keep the web browser open.
- **Compression**: For files like images, documents, or large collections, consider compressing them into a **ZIP file** before uploading. This reduces the size and ensures faster uploads.

- **Batch Uploading**: If you have multiple files to upload, select them all at once instead of uploading them individually. This can reduce the number of steps and allow Google Drive to handle them in bulk.

2. Creating and Organizing Folders

Creating New Folders

Organizing files into folders is one of the most effective ways to keep Google Drive manageable and easy to navigate.

1. **From Desktop (Web Version)**:
   - **Step 1**: In Google Drive, click the **+ New** button on the left-hand menu.
   - **Step 2**: Select **Folder** from the dropdown menu.

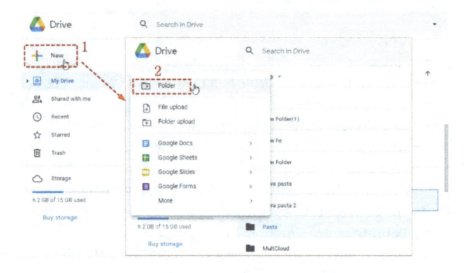

- Step 3: A small window will appear asking you to name your folder. Enter a name for the folder and click **Create**.

- Step 4: The folder will appear in your "My Drive." You can now drag and drop files into it, or right-click to move files into it.

2. **From Mobile (iOS/Android)**:
   - Step 1: Open the **Google Drive app** and tap the **+** icon in the bottom-right corner.
   - Step 2: Select **Folder**.
   - Step 3: Enter a name for your folder and tap **Create**.
   - Step 4: Once the folder is created, you can add files to it by selecting the files and choosing **Move to** to place them inside the folder.

Moving Files and Organizing Your Drive

After uploading files and creating folders, you may need to organize them by moving them around in Google Drive. Here's how:

1. **From Desktop (Web Version)**:
   - ○ **Step 1**: Select the file or folder you wish to move by clicking on it.
   - ○ **Step 2**: Right-click and select **Move to** from the context menu.
   - ○ **Step 3**: A file explorer window will open. Navigate to the desired folder or create a new folder by clicking the **+ New Folder** button.
   - ○ **Step 4**: Click **Move Here** to place the file in the selected folder.
2. **From Mobile (iOS/Android)**:
   - ○ **Step 1**: In the Google Drive app, tap and hold the file or folder you want to move.
   - ○ **Step 2**: Tap the **three-dot menu** and select **Move**.
   - ○ **Step 3**: Choose the target folder or create a new one by tapping the **+** icon and selecting **New Folder**.
   - ○ **Step 4**: Tap **Move Here** to place the file in the new folder.

Naming Conventions for Easy Organization

To help keep your Google Drive organized and make it easier to find specific files, adopting a consistent naming convention is key. Consider the following tips:

1. **Use Descriptive Names**: Always name files and folders with a clear description of their content. For example, instead of naming a file "Document1," use a name like "ProjectProposal_March2025."
2. **Include Dates**: Including dates in file names can help you easily sort files by year, month, or day. For example,

"MeetingMinutes_2025-03-10" is much more recognizable than "Minutes_March."

3. **Avoid Special Characters**: Google Drive doesn't allow certain special characters (like /, , *, or ?), so avoid using them in file or folder names.
4. **Use Prefixes**: You can use prefixes for further clarity, such as "Invoice_" for all invoices, or "Report_" for all reports.

3. File Search and Sorting

Using Google Drive's Search Bar

The **Search Bar** is one of the most powerful features in Google Drive, allowing you to locate files quickly. Here's how to use it effectively:

1. **Basic Search**: Simply type keywords into the search bar to find files by name or content.
2. **Search by File Type**: To search for specific types of files, enter keywords such as "doc," "pdf," or "jpg" in the search bar.
3. **Search by Owner**: If you're looking for files owned by someone else, type **owner: [name]** (e.g., "owner: John Doe") to find documents shared by that person.

Sorting and Filtering Files by Name, Date, Type, and More

Google Drive allows you to sort your files based on different criteria to make your search more efficient:

1. **Sort by Name**: In Google Drive, click the **Name** column header to sort files alphabetically.

2. **Sort by Date**: Click the **Last modified** column to sort files by when they were last edited. This can help you find recent files.

3. **Sort by File Type**: You can also sort by file type, like documents, spreadsheets, or images, by clicking on the **Type** column.

4. **Sort by Size**: If you want to find larger files to free up space, you can sort by file size.

Advanced Search Filters for Efficient File Location

Google Drive offers advanced search filters to refine your search and find files faster:

1. **File Type**: Click the drop-down arrow in the search bar to filter by file type, such as documents, spreadsheets, PDFs, and more.

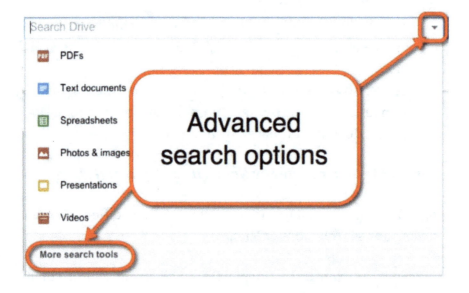

2. **Ownership**: Filter by **Owner** to find files created by a specific person, or use the "**Shared with me**" filter to find files that others have shared with you.
3. **Date Modified**: You can filter by date ranges, such as "Last 30 days," "Past Week," or a custom range.
4. **Has Keywords**: Use specific keywords to filter files that contain certain words, which is helpful when searching for text-heavy files.

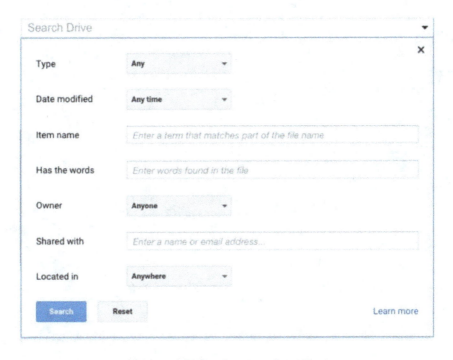

Click any of the dropdowns to select an item

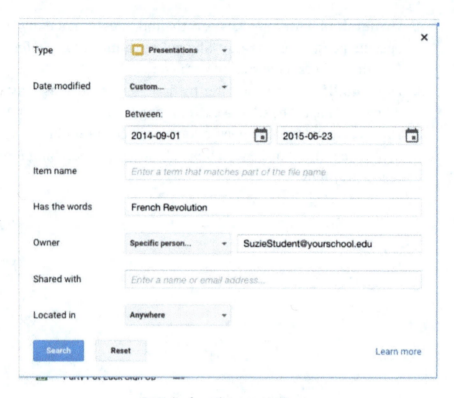

Example of search terms you can use

Chapter 3: Managing Files and Folders

1. Renaming, Moving, and Deleting Files

How to Rename Files and Folders

Renaming files and folders in Google Drive is straightforward and helps keep your storage organized. Here's how to rename files and folders:

1. **From Desktop (Web Version)**:
   - **Step 1**: Right-click on the file or folder you want to rename.
   - **Step 2**: From the context menu, select **Rename**.
   - **Step 3**: A text field will appear where you can edit the name of the file or folder. Type in the new name.
   - **Step 4**: Press **Enter** or click **OK** to confirm the new name.
2. **From Mobile (iOS/Android)**:
   - **Step 1**: Tap and hold the file or folder you want to rename.
   - **Step 2**: Tap the **three-dot menu** that appears.
   - **Step 3**: Select **Rename** from the options.
   - **Step 4**: Type the new name and tap **OK** or **Save**.

Renaming files and folders is a simple way to ensure that everything in your Google Drive is organized and easy to identify.

Moving Files into Different Folders

Organizing files into specific folders is crucial for managing your Google Drive effectively. Here's how you can move files:

1. **From Desktop (Web Version)**:
   - **Step 1**: Select the file or folder you want to move by clicking on it once.
   - **Step 2**: Right-click the file/folder and select **Move to** from the menu.
   - **Step 3**: A file explorer window will appear, showing all your folders in Google Drive.
   - **Step 4**: Browse through your folders, select the destination folder, and click **Move Here**.
2. **From Mobile (iOS/Android)**:
   - **Step 1**: In the Google Drive app, tap and hold the file or folder you wish to move.
   - **Step 2**: Tap the **three-dot menu** and select **Move**.
   - **Step 3**: Navigate to the folder where you want to move the file.
   - **Step 4**: Tap **Move Here** to place the file or folder in the new location.

Moving files into different folders is helpful for keeping related items together and ensuring better organization.

Deleting Files and Folders

Deleting unnecessary files or folders helps keep your Google Drive organized. Here's how to delete them:

1. **From Desktop (Web Version)**:

- o **Step 1**: Right-click the file or folder you want to delete.
- o **Step 2**: Click **Remove** from the context menu.
- o **Step 3**: The file will be moved to the **Trash** folder.
2. **From Mobile (iOS/Android)**:
   - o **Step 1**: Tap and hold the file or folder you want to delete.
   - o **Step 2**: Tap the **three-dot menu** and select **Remove**.
   - o **Step 3**: The file or folder will be moved to the Trash.

Deleted files aren't permanently deleted immediately, so you can still recover them if necessary.

Restoring Deleted Items from Trash

If you accidentally delete a file or folder, you can restore it from the Trash folder within 30 days.

1. **From Desktop (Web Version)**:
   - o **Step 1**: On the left sidebar, click on **Trash** to view deleted files.
   - o **Step 2**: Right-click the file or folder you want to restore.
   - o **Step 3**: Click **Restore** to move the file back to its original location.
2. **From Mobile (iOS/Android)**:
   - o **Step 1**: Open the **Google Drive app** and tap the **Menu** (three horizontal lines) in the top-left corner.
   - o **Step 2**: Select **Trash** from the menu.
   - o **Step 3**: Tap and hold the file you want to restore, then select **Restore**.

Files that are in the Trash are automatically deleted after 30 days, so make sure to restore important files before that time expires.

2. Version History

How to Access and View Version History

Google Drive automatically keeps track of all changes made to documents and files. This feature is called **Version History**, and it allows you to see edits made over time. Here's how to access and view it:

1. **From Desktop (Web Version)**:
   - o **Step 1**: Right-click the file for which you want to view version history and select **Version History** from the menu.
   - o **Step 2**: Click **See Version History**. A panel will appear on the right side of the screen.
   - o **Step 3**: The panel will show all previous versions of the file, with timestamps and the names of the users who made changes.
   - o **Step 4**: You can click any version to view it in its entirety.
2. **From Mobile (iOS/Android)**:
   - o **Note**: The version history feature is available in Google Docs, Sheets, and Slides, but not for other file types on the mobile app.
   - o **Step 1**: Open the document you wish to view the version history for.
   - o **Step 2**: Tap the **three-dot menu** in the top-right corner.

o   **Step 3**: Select **Version History** from the options. You can then see all the previous versions of the document.

Restoring Previous Versions of Files

If you need to revert a file to an earlier version, Google Drive makes it easy to restore it. Here's how:

1. **From Desktop (Web Version)**:
   o   **Step 1**: In the **Version History** panel (from the steps above), select the version you want to restore.
   o   **Step 2**: Click on the **three-dot menu** next to the version and select **Restore This Version**.
   o   **Step 3**: The file will be reverted to the selected version, and all changes will be undone.
2. **From Mobile (iOS/Android)**:
   o   **Note**: You can restore previous versions only in Google Docs, Sheets, and Slides.
   o   **Step 1**: Open the document you wish to restore.
   o   **Step 2**: Tap the **three-dot menu** in the top-right corner.
   o   **Step 3**: Tap **Version History**.
   o   **Step 4**: Select the version you want to restore, then choose **Restore This Version**.

Understanding Google Drive's Auto-Save Feature

One of the most powerful features of Google Drive is its **Auto-Save** functionality. Every time you make an edit in a Google Docs, Sheets, or Slides file, the changes are saved automatically in real-time, so there's no need to worry about losing your work.

- **Auto-Save in Google Docs/Sheets/Slides**: As you type or edit, Google Drive saves the file in the cloud continuously. The saved versions are automatically stored without requiring any manual intervention.
- **Working Offline**: If you're working offline (without an internet connection), your changes will be saved locally and synced to Google Drive once you reconnect to the internet.
- **No "Save" Button**: Unlike traditional applications, there is no need to click a **Save** button in Google Drive. Once your work is done, Google Drive automatically handles the saving process.

Chapter 4: Sharing and Collaborating in Google Drive

1. Sharing Files and Folders

How to Share Files and Folders via Email

Sharing files or folders via email is an effective way to collaborate, especially when you want to share specific files with individuals. Here's how to do it:

1. **From Desktop (Web Version)**:
    o   **Step 1**: Right-click on the file or folder you wish to share.
    o   **Step 2**: Select **Share** from the context menu.

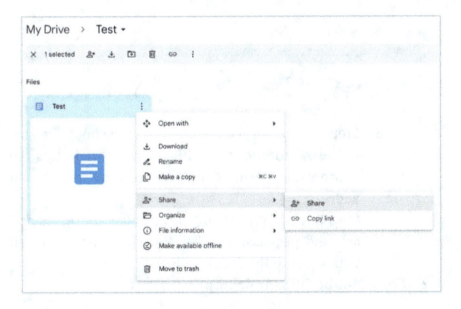

- o **Step 3**: A sharing window will appear. In the "Share with people and groups" section, enter the email addresses of the people you want to share the file with.

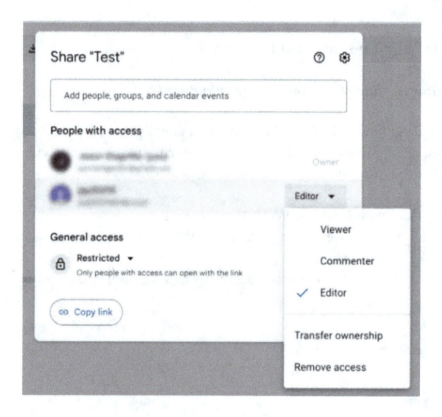

- o **Step 4**: You can choose whether they should be able to **View**, **Comment**, or **Edit** the file by selecting the appropriate permission level next to their email address.
- o **Step 5**: Once you've added the email addresses and selected permissions, click **Send** to send the email with a link to the file or folder.

2. **From Mobile (iOS/Android)**:

- o **Step 1**: Tap the three dots next to the file or folder you want to share.
- o **Step 2**: Tap **Share**.
- o **Step 3**: In the "Share with people" section, enter the email addresses of the people you want to share the file with.
- o **Step 4**: Set permissions (Viewer, Commenter, or Editor) by tapping the dropdown next to their email address.
- o **Step 5**: Tap **Send** to send an invitation to share the file or folder.

This method allows recipients to receive an email with direct access to the shared file or folder.

Setting Permissions: Viewer, Editor, Commenter

Google Drive provides three different permission levels when sharing files or folders:

1. **Viewer**: The person can only view the file or folder. They cannot make any changes or leave comments.
2. **Commenter**: The person can view the file and leave comments, but they cannot make any changes to the content.
3. **Editor**: The person can edit the file, make changes, and add or remove content. Editors also have the ability to share the file or folder with others, depending on the settings.

You can select these permissions during the sharing process to control the level of access that others have to your files.

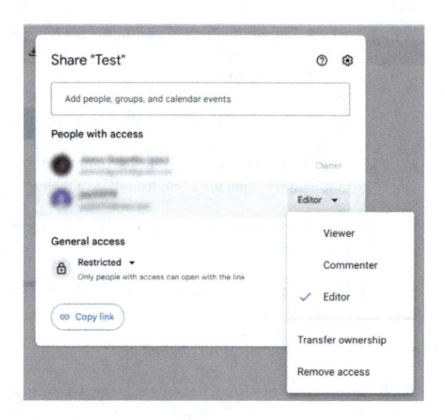

How to Share with Specific People or Groups

Google Drive allows you to share files or folders with specific people or groups by entering their email addresses.

1. **Step 1**: Click on the **Share** button for the file or folder.
2. **Step 2**: In the "Share with people and groups" section, type in the email addresses of the individuals or groups (Google Groups) you want to share the file with.
3. **Step 3**: Select the appropriate permission level (Viewer, Commenter, or Editor).
4. **Step 4**: Click **Send** to send the invitation.

If you have a Google Group set up, you can share the file with the group's email address, and all group members will automatically have access to the shared file or folder.

2. Advanced Sharing Options

Creating Shareable Links and Managing Access

Instead of emailing specific people, you can create a shareable link to your file or folder. Here's how:

1. **From Desktop (Web Version)**:
   o **Step 1**: Right-click the file or folder you want to share and select **Share**.

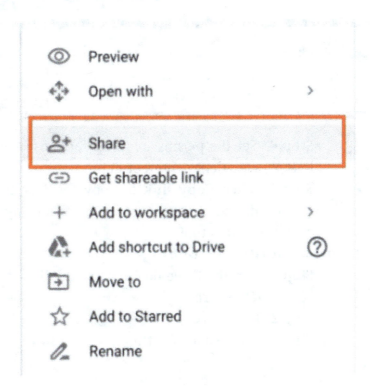

- o **Step 2**: In the sharing window, click on **Get link**.
- o **Step 3**: Choose your link sharing settings:
  - ▪ **Restricted**: Only people added explicitly can access the file.
  - ▪ **Anyone with the link**: Anyone who has the link can access the file.

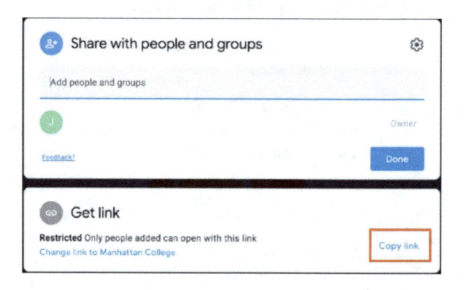

- o **Step 4**: Set the permission level for those with the link: Viewer, Commenter, or Editor.
- o **Step 5**: Click **Copy link** to copy the link to your clipboard, and share it through email or any other communication tool.

2. **From Mobile (iOS/Android)**:
   - o **Step 1**: Tap the three dots next to the file or folder you want to share.
   - o **Step 2**: Tap **Share**.
   - o **Step 3**: In the sharing settings, tap **Get link**.

- Step 4: Choose between restricted or anyone with the link settings.
- Step 5: Set the appropriate permissions for the link and tap **Copy link** to copy the shareable link.

Using a shareable link is convenient when you need to share a file with multiple people or want to provide easy access without sending individual invites.

Setting Expiration Dates for Links

You can set expiration dates for shared links to limit access after a certain period.

1. **From Desktop (Web Version)**:
   - Step 1: Right-click the file or folder and select **Share**.
   - Step 2: Click on **Get link**.
   - Step 3: Under "Anyone with the link," click the **down arrow** next to the access level, and select **Set expiration date**.

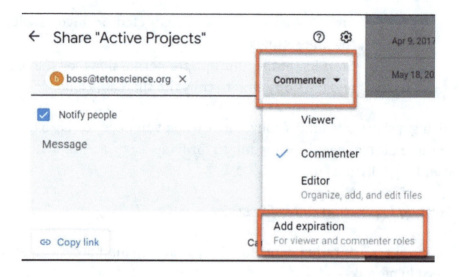

- Step 4: Choose the expiration date and click **Save**.
- Step 5: The link will automatically expire on the specified date.

Setting expiration dates is useful for temporary projects, file sharing for deadlines, or sensitive information that you don't want accessible indefinitely.

Collaborating with Non-Google Users

You can still share Google Drive files with people who don't have Google accounts. Here's how:

1. Step 1: Share the file by clicking **Share** and entering the email address of the non-Google user.
2. Step 2: When prompted, you'll be given the option to send them a link to access the file. They'll be able to view or comment on the file (depending on the permissions you've

set), but they won't be able to edit unless they have a Google account.

3. **Step 3**: Non-Google users can also download the file, view it in a web browser, or make comments (for supported file types like Docs, Sheets, and Slides).

For files that require collaboration, consider asking non-Google users to sign up for a Google account, which will give them full access to all collaboration features.

3. Real-Time Collaboration

Using Google Docs, Sheets, and Slides for Collaboration

Google Drive allows you to collaborate in real time on Google Docs, Sheets, and Slides. This means multiple people can edit or comment on the same document at the same time. Here's how to collaborate effectively:

1. **Step 1**: Open the Google Docs, Sheets, or Slides file you want to collaborate on.
2. **Step 2**: Share the file using the methods mentioned above.
3. **Step 3**: Once others join, you'll be able to see their cursor moving in real time, and any changes they make will be instantly visible to you.

Collaborating in real-time enhances productivity, allowing everyone to contribute and see updates as they happen.

Adding and Responding to Comments and Suggestions

Google Docs, Sheets, and Slides allow collaborators to leave comments or make suggestions, creating a dynamic environment for feedback. Here's how to add and respond:

1. **To Add a Comment**:
   - **Step 1**: Highlight the text or item you want to comment on.
   - **Step 2**: Right-click or click the **comment icon** (usually in the toolbar) and select **Comment**.

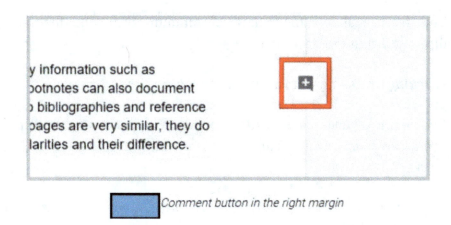

y information such as
ootnotes can also document
o bibliographies and reference
oages are very similar, they do
larities and their difference.

Comment button in the right margin

- o **Step 3**: Type your comment and click **Comment** to submit it.

2. **To Respond to a Comment**:
   - o **Step 1**: Click on the comment thread on the right panel.
   - o **Step 2**: Type your response in the box provided and press **Reply**.

This feature allows for seamless communication and feedback directly within the document.

Working on Documents Simultaneously

Google Drive enables **simultaneous editing**, meaning multiple users can work on a document at the same time. Here's how it works:

1. **Step 1**: Share the document with the people you want to collaborate with.
2. **Step 2**: As they start editing, you'll see their changes instantly. Each person's cursor will be highlighted in a different color, making it easy to see who is working on what.
3. **Step 3**: You can also chat directly within the document using the **comment section** or use **suggesting mode** to make non-destructive changes that the owner or collaborators can accept or reject.

Simultaneous editing streamlines the collaboration process, making it efficient for teams working on shared files.

Chapter 5: Google Drive on Mobile Devices

1. Using the Google Drive App

Uploading Files from Mobile Devices

Uploading files to Google Drive from a mobile device is simple and allows you to easily store your documents, photos, videos, and more. Here's how to upload files using the Google Drive app:

1. **Step 1**: Open the **Google Drive app** on your mobile device.
2. **Step 2**: Tap the **"+" button** (usually at the bottom right of the screen).
3. **Step 3**: Select **Upload** from the options that appear.
4. **Step 4**: Choose the type of file you wish to upload (e.g., photos, videos, documents).
   - **For Photos and Videos**: Tap on the **Gallery** or **Photos** option, select the files you want to upload, and confirm by tapping **Upload**.
   - **For Documents**: Navigate to the file storage location on your device, select the document(s), and upload them.
5. **Step 5**: The file will begin uploading to your Google Drive and can be accessed across all devices where you're signed in to Google Drive.

Uploading files from your mobile device gives you the flexibility to back up files and share them anytime, anywhere.

Managing Files and Folders on Mobile

Once files are uploaded, you can manage them using the Google Drive app:

1. **Navigating Files and Folders**:
   - The main screen of the app will display all your files and folders. You can scroll through them, tap to open, or use the **search bar** at the top to find specific items.
2. **Creating Folders**:
   - To create a new folder, tap the **"+" button** and select **Folder**. Enter a name for the folder and tap **Create**.
3. **Moving and Organizing Files**:
   - To move files, tap and hold the file you want to move, then select **Move** from the menu. Choose the destination folder and tap **Move here**.
4. **Renaming Files**:
   - Tap and hold the file, then select **Rename**. Enter the new file name and tap **OK** to save changes.
5. **Deleting Files**:
   - Tap and hold the file, then select **Remove**. This will move the file to the **Trash**, from where it can be permanently deleted or restored later.
6. **Sorting Files**:
   - You can sort files by name, date, or size by tapping the **three dots** (menu) icon at the top of the screen, selecting **Sort**, and choosing your preferred method.

Managing files and folders on your mobile device is straightforward and ensures that you can stay organized, even when on the go.

Offline Access and File Syncing

The Google Drive app allows you to access your files offline, which is particularly useful when you're traveling or in areas with limited internet connectivity. Here's how to manage offline access:

1. **Enabling Offline Mode for Files**:
    - o **Step 1**: Open the Google Drive app and find the file you want to access offline.
    - o **Step 2**: Tap and hold the file, then select **Available offline** from the menu. The file will be downloaded and available without an internet connection.
2. **Managing Offline Files**:
    - o To see which files are available offline, tap the **Menu icon** (three horizontal lines) in the top left, then go to **Offline**. All files set for offline access will be listed here.
3. **Syncing Files**:
    - o When you're online again, any changes made to offline files will automatically sync to your Google Drive once you have a connection. Be sure to check that your files have synced successfully before offline work, as this ensures all your changes are backed up.

Offline access allows you to work on your files anytime, even without an internet connection. Once connected, your files will automatically sync to the cloud.

2. Editing Files on Mobile Devices

Editing Google Docs, Sheets, and Slides on the Go

The Google Drive mobile app supports editing Google Docs, Sheets, and Slides files directly on your device. Here's how to edit them:

1. **Step 1**: Open the **Google Drive app** and navigate to the file you want to edit.
2. **Step 2**: Tap on the file (Google Docs, Sheets, or Slides) to open it.
   - For **Google Docs**, you can type directly into the document.
   - For **Google Sheets**, you can edit cells, add data, and use formulas.
   - For **Google Slides**, you can add, delete, or edit slides and text boxes.
3. **Step 3**: All changes are saved automatically as you make edits. The app functions similarly to the web version, with real-time syncing when you are online.

Editing files on the go allows for productivity without needing a laptop or desktop, ensuring that you can work from virtually anywhere.

Managing Offline Files and Syncing Back

If you have enabled offline access for your files, you can continue editing documents even when you're not connected to the internet. Here's how to manage offline edits:

1. **Step 1**: Ensure that the file you wish to edit is available offline (as described above).
2. **Step 2**: Open the file in the **Google Docs**, **Google Sheets**, or **Google Slides** app and make your edits as needed.

3. **Step 3**: Once you have an internet connection, your changes will automatically sync back to Google Drive.
    - The sync happens in the background, so you don't need to do anything extra.
    - **Note**: If you edit the same document from multiple devices (e.g., from your phone and desktop), Google Drive will automatically merge the changes and keep everything up-to-date.

Offline editing ensures you remain productive even in areas with limited or no internet access. Once you're back online, all the changes you made will sync back to your cloud storage, keeping everything updated across your devices.

Chapter 6: Google Docs, Sheets, and Slides in Google Drive

1. Using Google Docs in Drive

Creating, Editing, and Formatting Documents

Google Docs allows you to create, edit, and format documents directly within Google Drive. Here's how to get started:

1. **Creating a New Document**:
   - **Step 1**: Open **Google Drive** and click the **"+" button** in the lower right corner of the screen.
   - **Step 2**: Select **Google Docs** from the menu. This will create a new, blank document.

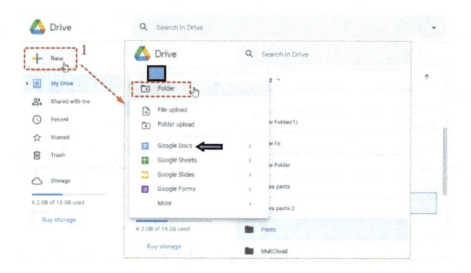

o **Step 3**: Begin typing your content. Google Docs will automatically save your document as you work.

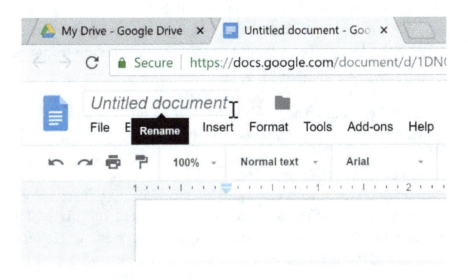

2. **Editing a Document**:
   o **Step 1**: Open an existing Google Doc by clicking on it in your Google Drive.
   o **Step 2**: You can edit the text, change formatting, or make any other changes directly within the document.
   o **Step 3**: Google Docs automatically saves all changes in real time, so you don't need to worry about manually saving your work.
3. **Formatting Your Document**:
   o Google Docs offers a wide range of formatting options, such as **font styles**, **text sizes**, **colors**, **bold**, **italics**, and **underlining**.

o You can format paragraphs using alignment options (left, right, center, justified), change line spacing, and use bulleted or numbered lists.

o To apply formatting, highlight the text you want to modify and choose the appropriate option from the toolbar at the top.

By using these simple editing and formatting tools, you can create professional-looking documents directly from Google Drive.

Using Templates in Google Docs

Google Docs also offers a range of **pre-designed templates** for creating various types of documents, such as resumes, letters, reports, and more. Here's how to use them:

1. **Step 1**: Open Google Docs in Google Drive.
2. **Step 2**: Click the **Template Gallery** button at the top of the screen.
3. **Step 3**: Browse through available templates, which are organized into categories like **Resumes, Letters, Reports**, etc.
4. **Step 4**: Select the template that best fits your needs. A new document will be created with the selected template.
5. **Step 5**: Customize the template by editing the text and adjusting formatting as needed.

Using templates can save you time and help you create well-structured documents without needing to start from scratch.

2. Google Sheets for Beginners

Creating, Formatting, and Working with Spreadsheets

Google Sheets allows you to create and manage spreadsheets for various tasks, such as data analysis, budgeting, and more. Here's how to get started:

1. **Creating a New Spreadsheet**:
   - **Step 1**: In Google Drive, click the **"+" button** and select **Google Sheets** to create a blank spreadsheet.
   - **Step 2**: Start entering your data into the cells. You can click on any cell and type in the content (numbers, text, etc.).
2. **Formatting Your Spreadsheet**:
   - Google Sheets offers many formatting options for cells, rows, and columns.
   - To format text in cells, highlight the text and use the toolbar at the top to change the font size, color, and alignment.
   - You can also adjust the width and height of rows and columns by clicking and dragging the borders.
3. **Working with Multiple Sheets**:
   - You can add multiple sheets (tabs) within a single Google Sheets file. To add a new sheet, click the **"+"** symbol at the bottom left of the screen.
   - You can switch between sheets by clicking on their respective tabs at the bottom of the file.

Creating and formatting spreadsheets in Google Sheets is easy and intuitive, making it a great tool for beginners.

Basic Formulas and Functions

One of the most powerful features of Google Sheets is the ability to perform calculations using formulas and functions. Here are the basics:

1. **Simple Addition**:
   - In any cell, type **=A1+B1** to add the values in cells A1 and B1.
2. **Using SUM**:
   - To sum a range of cells, type **=SUM(A1:A5)** to add the values from cells A1 through A5.
3. **Using AVERAGE**:
   - To find the average of a range, type **=AVERAGE(A1:A5)** to calculate the average of values in cells A1 through A5.
4. **Using IF Function**:
   - The **IF** function allows you to perform conditional calculations. For example, type **=IF(A1>10, "Yes", "No")** to check if the value in cell A1 is greater than 10. If it is, the cell will display **Yes**, otherwise **No**.
5. **Basic Date and Time Functions**:
   - Use **=TODAY()** to display the current date.
   - Use **=NOW()** to display the current date and time.

These basic formulas and functions will help you perform essential calculations in Google Sheets and make your spreadsheets more dynamic.

3. Google Slides for Presentations

Creating and Formatting Presentations

Google Slides is a powerful tool for creating presentations. Here's how to get started with creating and formatting slides:

1. **Creating a New Presentation**:
    - **Step 1**: Open Google Drive and click the **"+" button**.
    - **Step 2**: Select **Google Slides** to create a new blank presentation.
2. **Adding Slides**:
    - To add a new slide, click the **"+" button** or press **Ctrl+M** (Windows) or **Cmd+M** (Mac).
    - You can also duplicate a slide by selecting a slide and clicking **Ctrl+D** (Windows) or **Cmd+D** (Mac).
3. **Formatting Your Presentation**:
    - Google Slides offers a variety of formatting tools for both slides and text.
    - To format text, use the toolbar at the top to change font styles, sizes, colors, and alignments.
    - You can also change the background color of a slide or apply a theme by clicking **Slide** in the top menu and selecting **Change background**.

Adding Text, Images, and Transitions

1. **Adding Text**:
    - Click on a text box and start typing your content. You can resize the text box by dragging its corners.

- You can format text within the text box using the formatting toolbar at the top.

2. **Adding Images**:
   - To insert an image, click on **Insert** in the top menu, then select **Image**. You can upload an image from your computer, Google Drive, or search the web for an image.
   - You can resize and move the image on the slide by clicking and dragging its corners.

3. **Adding Transitions**:
   - Click on the **Slide** menu, then select **Transition**.
   - Choose a transition style (e.g., **Fade**, **Slide from right**) and apply it to all slides or specific slides.
   - You can also adjust the speed of transitions and apply animations to text and objects on the slide.

These tools allow you to create engaging, well-designed presentations for any occasion.

Chapter 7: Backing Up and Syncing with Google Drive

1. Setting Up Google Backup and Sync

Downloading and Installing Google Backup and Sync

Google Backup and Sync is a powerful tool for automatically syncing files between your computer and Google Drive. Here's how to download and set it up:

1. **Step 1: Download Google Backup and Sync:**
   - Visit the official Google Drive website.
   - Scroll down to the "Personal" section and click **Download** under "Backup and Sync."
   - A setup file will be downloaded to your computer.
2. **Step 2: Install Google Backup and Sync:**
   - Once the file has finished downloading, locate and open the setup file.
   - Follow the on-screen instructions to install the software. The installer will guide you through the process.
   - After installation, the **Backup and Sync** application will launch automatically.
3. **Step 3: Sign in with Your Google Account:**
   - Once the software is installed, sign in with your Google Account credentials. This will link Backup and Sync with your Google Drive account.

By completing these steps, you will have Google Backup and Sync installed and connected to your Google Drive account.

Syncing Files Between Your Computer and Google Drive

Once Backup and Sync is installed, you can easily sync files between your local computer and Google Drive. Here's how to configure syncing:

1. **Step 1: Select Folders to Sync**:
   - After signing into Backup and Sync, a setup window will appear asking you to choose which folders you want to sync with Google Drive.
   - You can choose to sync everything in your **Google Drive**, or you can select specific folders on your computer to sync.
   - To choose which folders to sync, click the checkboxes next to the folders you want to include in the sync.
2. **Step 2: Sync Files from Google Drive to Your Computer**:
   - By default, Backup and Sync will sync all your files and folders from Google Drive to your computer.
   - If you want to sync only specific folders from Google Drive, click on the **Advanced Settings** and select which folders to sync.
   - Any files or folders added to Google Drive will automatically be synced to your local computer.
3. **Step 3: Accessing Files Locally**:
   - After syncing, you can access your Google Drive files directly from your computer's **File Explorer** (Windows) or **Finder** (Mac). These files will be stored in a folder called **Google Drive**.

With this setup, your files will be automatically synced between your local computer and Google Drive. This means that changes made on your computer or in Google Drive will be reflected across both locations.

How to Choose Which Files to Sync

You have control over which files and folders to sync between your computer and Google Drive. Here's how to adjust these settings:

1. **Step 1: Open Google Backup and Sync Preferences**:
    o Click on the **Backup and Sync** icon in your system tray (Windows) or menu bar (Mac).
    o Click on the three vertical dots (more options) and select **Preferences**.

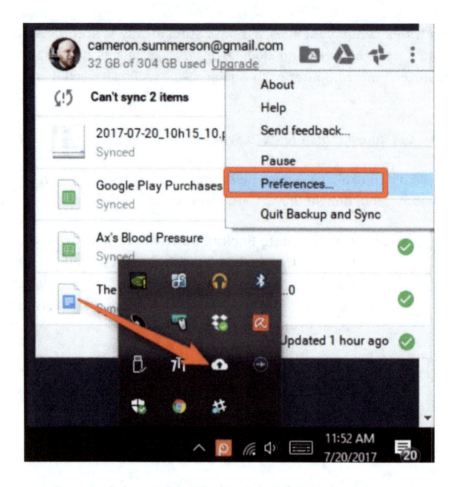

2. **Step 2: Select Which Folders to Sync**:
   o Under the **Google Drive** section, you can choose to sync all of your files or only specific folders.
   o To sync only certain folders, select **Sync only these folders** and check the boxes next to the folders you want to sync.
   o You can also manage what gets synced under the **My Computer** section by selecting which local folders to sync with Google Drive.

3. **Step 3: Save Preferences**:
    - After choosing the folders to sync, click **OK** to save your preferences. The selected files and folders will now sync between your computer and Google Drive.

By adjusting these settings, you can control exactly which files and folders are synced, saving space on your device and optimizing your backup.

2. Managing Synced Files

How to Sync Folders and Files Across Multiple Devices

One of the key benefits of Google Drive is that you can sync files across multiple devices. Here's how to manage file syncing between different computers and devices:

1. **Step 1: Set Up Google Backup and Sync on Other Devices**:
    - Repeat the installation process for **Backup and Sync** on each device (computer or mobile) that you want to sync.
    - Sign in with the same Google Account on each device to ensure they are linked.
2. **Step 2: Choose Which Files to Sync**:
    - On each device, you can choose which files or folders to sync from Google Drive. To do this, follow the same process as outlined earlier in **Setting Up Google Backup and Sync**.
    - Choose to sync specific folders based on your device's available storage and your usage needs.
3. **Step 3: Syncing Across Devices**:

- Once synced, any changes you make on one device will automatically be reflected on all other devices.
- For example, if you add a file on your desktop, that file will automatically appear on your mobile device (and vice versa) as long as both devices are connected to the internet.

By syncing files across multiple devices, you ensure that your important files are available to you anywhere, at any time.

Troubleshooting Syncing Issues

If syncing issues arise, here are some common solutions to fix them:

1. **Check Internet Connection**:
   - Syncing requires a stable internet connection. Ensure that your devices are connected to the internet.
   - If you have a weak or intermittent connection, it may cause syncing to fail.
2. **Pause and Resume Syncing**:
   - If syncing is slow or stuck, try pausing and resuming it.
   - Click on the **Backup and Sync** icon, and select **Pause** to stop syncing temporarily. Then, click **Resume** to restart the process.
3. **Ensure Sufficient Storage Space**:
   - Google Drive and your local device need enough storage space to sync files. If either has insufficient space, syncing may be interrupted.
   - Free up space on your device or Google Drive if necessary.

4. **Update Backup and Sync**:
   - Ensure you have the latest version of **Backup and Sync**. If not, go to the official Google website to download and install the newest version.
5. **Re-login to Google Account**:
   - If syncing stops or errors persist, log out of **Backup and Sync** and sign in again with your Google Account credentials.
6. **Check for File-Specific Issues**:
   - Large or unsupported files may not sync correctly. Ensure that files you are trying to sync are supported by Google Drive and check if they are too large to upload.
7. **Check Google Drive Storage Limits**:
   - If your Google Drive storage is full, new files cannot sync. Go to your Google Drive storage settings to see how much space you have left. You may need to free up space or purchase more storage.

By troubleshooting these common syncing issues, you can ensure that your files stay backed up and accessible across all devices.

Chapter 8: Securing Your Files in Google Drive

1. Google Drive Security Features

Understanding File and Folder Privacy

Google Drive offers various security measures to keep your files and folders safe. Here's how to manage the privacy of your files:

1. **File Ownership**:
   - Every file in Google Drive has an **owner**. The owner is the person who uploaded or created the file. The owner has full control over the file and can set its sharing permissions.
   - As the file owner, you can control who has access to the file and what kind of permissions they have.
2. **File Sharing Settings**:
   - By default, files are private to the owner. However, you can change the privacy settings by adjusting the file's sharing permissions. You can choose to share files with specific people, groups, or make them publicly accessible with a shareable link.
3. **Preventing Unauthorized Access**:
   - Ensure that only trusted individuals have access to sensitive files. You can restrict access by setting specific permissions and removing access for people who no longer need it.

4. **Folder Privacy**:
    o The same sharing and privacy settings apply to folders in Google Drive. If you share a folder, all files within that folder will inherit the folder's sharing settings. Make sure to review folder sharing settings if you want different files to have different levels of access.

Enabling Two-Factor Authentication (2FA)

Two-factor authentication (2FA) adds an extra layer of security to your Google Drive account. It requires you to provide two forms of verification to access your account: your password and a second factor, such as a code sent to your phone. Here's how to enable 2FA:

1. **Step 1: Go to Google Account Settings**:
    o Open your web browser and go to Google Account at https://myaccount.google.com/
    o Click on the **Security** tab on the left-hand sidebar.

2. **Step 2: Enable 2-Step Verification**:

- Scroll down to the **Signing in to Google** section and select **2-Step Verification**.
- Click **Get Started** to begin the setup process.
3. **Step 3: Set Up the Second Verification Method**:
   - You will be prompted to enter your password.
   - Google will ask you to choose a second form of verification:
     - **Google Prompts**: A prompt will be sent to your mobile device for easy access.
     - **Text Message/Phone Call**: A verification code will be sent to your phone.
     - **Authenticator App**: Use an app like Google Authenticator to generate a unique code for login.

4. **Step 4: Confirm Your 2FA Setup**:
   - Once you've set up the second form of verification, Google will confirm that 2-Step Verification is enabled.

o   From now on, every time you log into your Google Account, you will be asked for your password and the second verification code.

2FA significantly enhances the security of your Google Drive, ensuring that only you can access your files, even if your password is compromised.

2. Managing File Permissions and Access

Controlling Who Has Access to Your Files

Google Drive offers multiple ways to control who has access to your files, allowing you to share files securely. Here's how to manage access:

1. **Step 1: Open the File's Sharing Settings**:
    o   Right-click on a file or folder in Google Drive and select **Share.**
    o   The **Share with others** window will open.
2. **Step 2: Add People or Groups**:
    o   In the **Share with people and groups** field, enter the email addresses of the individuals or groups you want to share the file with.
    o   You can also select people from your Google Contacts.
3. **Step 3: Choose Permissions for Each User**:
    o   **Viewer**: The person can only view the file.
    o   **Commenter**: The person can view and leave comments on the file but cannot edit it.
    o   **Editor**: The person can view, edit, and comment on the file.

4. **Step 4: Send Invitation**:
   - ○ After selecting the appropriate permissions for each individual, click **Send** to share the file.
   - ○ The recipients will receive an email with a link to access the file or folder.

By controlling who has access to your files, you ensure that only authorized people can view, edit, or comment on your documents.

Setting Access Levels: Owner, Editor, Viewer, Commenter

Google Drive allows you to set specific access levels to ensure the right individuals have the right amount of control over your files. Here's a breakdown of each access level:

1. **Owner**:
   - ○ The **owner** of the file has complete control over it. They can edit, delete, and share the file with others.
   - ○ Only the owner can transfer ownership to another person.
   - ○ If you're the owner of a file, you have the ability to change the file's permissions for others.
2. **Editor**:
   - ○ An **editor** can edit the content of the file, comment on it, and share it with others. However, editors cannot remove the owner or change ownership.
   - ○ Editors have full control over the content of the file, but they cannot modify its fundamental permissions or ownership settings.
3. **Viewer**:

- A **viewer** can only view the file. They cannot make any changes or leave comments.
- Viewers can download, print, or copy the file (unless restricted by the owner).

4. **Commenter**:
   - A **commenter** can leave comments on the file, but they cannot edit its content.
   - Commenters can view and comment, but they cannot modify the file itself.

By selecting the appropriate access level for each individual, you can ensure that your files are shared securely and only with the right level of access.

Understanding Shared Drives and Permissions

Google Drive offers a feature called **Shared Drives** (formerly Team Drives), which is useful for collaborative teams. Here's how to understand and manage permissions for Shared Drives:

1. **Step 1: Creating a Shared Drive**:
   - In Google Drive, click on **Shared Drives** in the left-hand sidebar.
   - Click **+ New** to create a new shared drive.
   - Name the drive and choose who will have access to it.

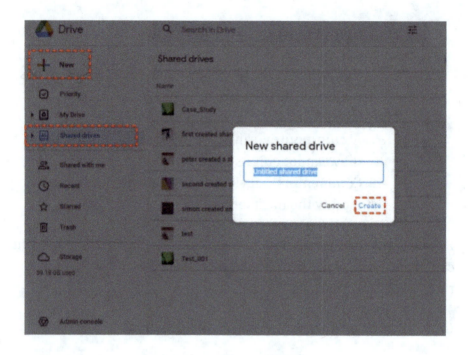

2. **Step 2: Setting Permissions in Shared Drives**:

   - **Manager**: The manager can add and remove members, change permissions, and manage settings for the shared drive.
   - **Content Manager**: Content managers can add, edit, and organize files, but they cannot manage settings or people.
   - **Contributor**: Contributors can add and edit files in the shared drive, but they cannot delete files or manage settings.
   - **Commenter**: Commenters can view and comment on files but cannot edit them.
   - **Viewer**: Viewers can only view files within the shared drive.

3. **Step 3: Managing Permissions for Shared Drive Members**:

   o To assign roles to members, click on **Manage members** in the shared drive settings.

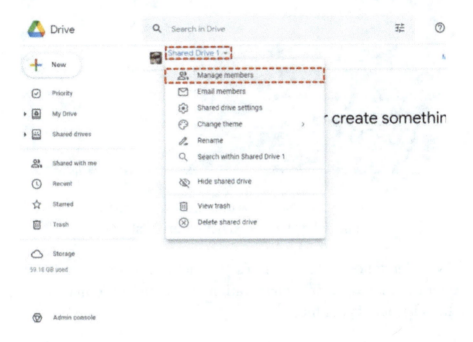

   o Add people or groups, and select their role (Manager, Content Manager, Contributor, Commenter, or Viewer).

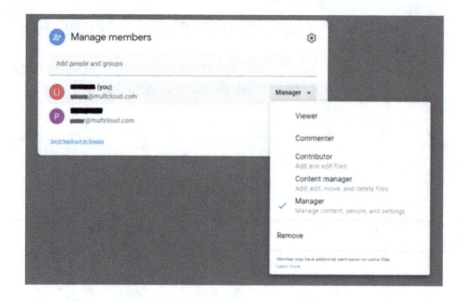

- o You can also allow members to share files outside the shared drive or restrict external sharing.

By understanding Shared Drives and their associated permissions, you can manage team collaboration efficiently while maintaining the security of your files.

Chapter 9: Storage Management in Google Drive

1. How Much Storage Do You Get for Free?

Understanding Google Drive's Free Storage Limit

When you sign up for a Google account, you automatically get access to Google Drive and a generous amount of free storage. Here's what you need to know:

1. **Google's Free Storage Offer**:
   - Every Google account comes with **15 GB of free storage** shared across Google Drive, Gmail, and Google Photos.
   - This storage is available to store files, emails, and attachments, as well as any photos and videos that are backed up through Google Photos.
2. **Storage Breakdown**:
   - **Google Drive**: Files such as documents, presentations, spreadsheets, and PDFs contribute to your free storage limit.
   - **Gmail**: Emails and their attachments are stored in your Google Drive storage quota. Be mindful that large attachments can fill up your storage quickly.
   - **Google Photos**: Photos and videos uploaded in original quality also count toward your storage limit. However, if you upload images in "Storage saver"

(previously known as "High quality"), they no longer count toward your storage limit, but this may change, so it's important to review Google's current policies.

3. **How Storage is Used**:
   - While Google Docs, Sheets, and Slides don't count toward your storage limit, files that are converted to these formats from non-Google formats (like PDFs or Word documents) do.
   - Keep in mind that the 15 GB is a combined storage limit across all services.

What Happens When You Reach the Storage Limit?

Once you reach the 15 GB storage limit, you will no longer be able to upload new files, send or receive emails, or back up new photos and videos. Here's what happens next:

1. **Notifications**:
   - Google will notify you when you're close to reaching the storage limit. You'll also get a warning when you hit the limit.
2. **Effects of Reaching the Limit**:
   - **Google Drive**: You won't be able to upload new files or save changes to existing files.
   - **Gmail**: You won't be able to send or receive new emails. Emails you try to send will remain in your outbox.
   - **Google Photos**: Any new photos or videos you try to upload will be blocked.
3. **Options to Free Up Space**:

o   If you're near or at your storage limit, you can either delete files to free up space or purchase additional storage through **Google One**.

2. Managing Storage

How to Check Your Storage Usage

Knowing how much storage you've used is crucial for managing your space. Here's how you can check your Google Drive storage usage:

1. **Step 1: Access Storage Information**:
    o   Open Google Drive on the web by visiting drive.google.com.
    o   In the bottom left corner, you'll see your storage usage displayed as a progress bar. Click on this to view detailed storage information.

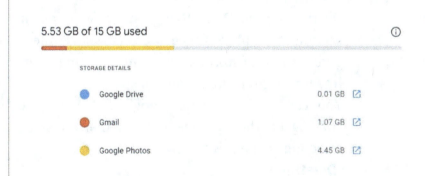

2. **Step 2: Check Storage Breakdown**:

o You'll be redirected to the **Google One** storage page, where you can see the breakdown of how your storage is used across Google Drive, Gmail, and Google Photos.

3. **Step 3: Detailed Storage Information**:
    o Here you can see exactly how much storage is used by:
        ▪ Google Drive (including all files and folders)
        ▪ Gmail (emails and attachments)
        ▪ Google Photos (photos and videos)
    o This detailed information helps you pinpoint where you might need to free up space.

Cleaning Up and Deleting Files to Free Up Space

To manage your storage and prevent hitting your limit, regularly clean up your Google Drive by deleting unnecessary files. Here's how to free up space:

1. **Step 1: Identify Large Files**:
    o On the **Google One storage page**, you can find a section that shows **large files**. These are files that take up a lot of storage space, and deleting them can free up a significant amount of space.
    o You can also sort your Google Drive by size by clicking on the **Storage** link on the left side and selecting **Large Files**.
2. **Step 2: Deleting Files**:
    o Once you've identified unnecessary files, you can delete them by right-clicking on the file or folder and selecting **Remove**.

o Deleted files will be moved to the **Trash**.

3. **Step 3: Emptying the Trash**:
   o Deleted files still take up storage space until they're permanently removed. To do this:
      ▪ Go to the **Trash** in Google Drive (found in the left sidebar).
      ▪ Select **Empty Trash** to permanently delete the files and free up space.

4. **Step 4: Reviewing Gmail and Google Photos**:
   o **Gmail**: Delete old emails with large attachments by searching for emails with attachments, or use filters like **larger:10MB** to find larger emails. Once deleted, make sure to empty your Gmail Trash.
   o **Google Photos**: Check for large photos or videos that you may no longer need. Consider deleting unnecessary or duplicate photos/videos to free up space.

By cleaning up your Google Drive, Gmail, and Google Photos, you can significantly reduce your storage usage and stay under the free limit.

3. Upgrading Storage with Google One

Overview of Google One Subscription

If you find yourself consistently hitting the storage limit, you can upgrade your storage by subscribing to **Google One**. Google One is a subscription service that gives you additional storage across Google Drive, Gmail, and Google Photos.

1. **Google One Features**:
    - Google One offers **more storage** with plans ranging from 100 GB to 30 TB.
    - With Google One, you can get access to premium support, such as help from Google experts, and additional benefits like **family sharing** (up to 5 family members can share the storage plan).

How to Upgrade Storage

1. **Step 1: Choose Your Plan**:
    - To upgrade, visit the Google One website or open the **Google One** app.
    - Review the available storage plans:
        - **100 GB** plan: Suitable for basic users who need more than the free 15 GB.
        - **200 GB, 2 TB, or more**: Choose larger plans if you have many files, emails, or photos to store.
2. **Step 2: Subscribe**:
    - Select the plan that best suits your needs, and follow the instructions to purchase the subscription. You'll need to provide payment information (credit card or PayPal).
3. **Step 3: Enjoy Extra Storage**:
    - After subscribing, your storage across Google Drive, Gmail, and Google Photos will automatically increase to your new storage limit.
    - Your Google One plan will renew automatically each month or year, depending on your subscription preference.

Benefits of Google One Plans

1. **More Storage**:
   - The primary benefit of Google One is **additional storage**, which can be shared with your family members.
2. **Enhanced Support**:
   - Google One subscribers have access to **premium support**. This means you can get direct help from Google experts for any issues related to your Google services.
3. **Family Sharing**:
   - With Google One, you can share your plan with up to 5 family members, each with their own private storage. This is especially useful for families with multiple users who need storage for their documents, photos, and emails.
4. **Other Benefits**:
   - Subscribers may also get additional benefits like discounts on Google products or services, and sometimes even free trials of other services.

By understanding your free storage limit, checking your storage usage regularly, and upgrading to Google One if necessary, you can effectively manage your Google Drive storage and ensure you never run out of space for your important files.

Chapter 10: Recovering Files in Google Drive

1. Google Drive Trash and File Recovery

How to Recover Files from Trash

Google Drive has a built-in Trash feature where deleted files and folders are temporarily stored. If you've accidentally deleted something, don't worry—it's likely still recoverable! Here's how you can restore files from Trash:

1. **Step 1: Access the Trash**:
    o   On the **Google Drive** web interface, click on **Trash** in the left sidebar.

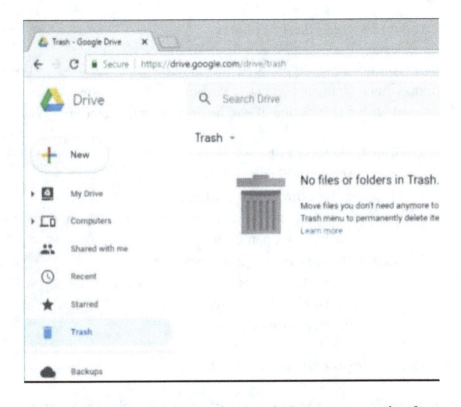

Trash - Google Drive

Secure | https://drive.google.com/drive/trash

△ Drive

Q Search Drive

Trash ▾

╋ New

▸ 🖵 My Drive

▸ 🖵 Computers

👥 Shared with me

🕓 Recent

★ Starred

🗑 Trash

☁ Backups

No files or folders in Trash.

Move files you don't need anymore to Trash menu to permanently delete ite Learn more

- o On mobile, open the Google Drive app, tap the **three-line menu** (hamburger menu) in the top left corner, and then tap **Trash**.
2. **Step 2: Find the Deleted File**:
   - o Browse through the Trash folder to locate the file or folder you want to recover. Files are organized by their deletion date, with the most recently deleted items at the top.
3. **Step 3: Restore the File**:
   - o Right-click on the file (or tap and hold on mobile) and select **Restore**.
   - o The file will be restored to its original location in Google Drive.

Restoring Deleted Files or Folders

When you delete a file or folder in Google Drive, it moves to the Trash, where you can recover it within **30 days**. If the file is not restored within this period, it will be permanently deleted.

1. **Step 1: Go to Trash**:
   - Access the **Trash** folder in Google Drive.
2. **Step 2: Select the File or Folder**:
   - Once you find the deleted item, right-click on it or tap and hold to open options.
3. **Step 3: Restore to Original Location**:
   - Choose the **Restore** option to recover the item. It will return to the same location in your Google Drive it was in before deletion.

Understanding Google Drive's Trash Policy

Here's what you need to know about Google Drive's Trash feature:

1. **Automatic Deletion**:
   - Files and folders in Trash are automatically deleted after **30 days**. Once deleted, the items are gone permanently and cannot be recovered.
2. **Storage Impact**:
   - Items in Trash still count toward your storage quota. To free up space, remember to empty Trash after deleting unnecessary files.
3. **Restoring Files After 30 Days**:

o   After the 30-day period, items in Trash are permanently deleted. At that point, you cannot recover them through the Trash folder.

2. Using Google Drive Rewind

What is Google Drive Rewind?

Google Drive Rewind is a powerful feature that allows you to revert your entire Google Drive to a previous version, which can be useful if something went wrong and you want to restore your files to a specific point in time. This feature can be particularly helpful in situations like mass accidental deletions, file corruption, or errors caused by third-party apps.

1. **How It Works**:
    o   Google Drive stores version histories for files, and Rewind can undo changes to your entire Drive, restoring all your files to a state from earlier in the day, week, or month.
    o   This is similar to restoring individual file versions, but Rewind affects all the files and folders in your Google Drive account.

Restoring Your Entire Google Drive to a Previous Version

1. **Step 1: Access the Google Drive Settings**:
    o   Go to the **Google Drive web interface** at drive.google.com.
    o   Click on the **Settings** gear icon in the upper-right corner and select **Settings**.

2. **Step 2: Open the "Manage Versions" or "Activity" Section**:
   - o   In the settings menu, navigate to the **Activity** section where you can track changes across your Drive. This will show you all actions taken on your files and folders, such as edits, deletions, or new uploads.
3. **Step 3: Using Google Drive Rewind**:
   - o   From the **Activity** view, you can use the **Rewind** feature to restore files to a previous state. You can select a date from the **timeline** of activity to revert all files and folders in your Drive back to that point.
   - o   **Important Note**: This will restore all files in your Drive to their previous states, so any changes made after the selected date will be undone.
4. **Step 4: Confirm Rewind**:
   - o   After selecting the desired time and date, confirm that you want to revert your Drive to this earlier version.
   - o   Once confirmed, Google Drive will begin the process of restoring your files.
5. **Step 5: Check the Restored Files**:
   - o   Once the process is complete, go back to your Drive and verify that the files have been restored to their correct versions.

Chapter 11: Integrating Google Drive with Other Google Services

1. Using Google Drive with Gmail

Attaching Google Drive Files to Emails

Google Drive seamlessly integrates with Gmail, allowing you to attach files directly from your Google Drive storage to your emails. Here's how you can do it:

1. **Step 1: Open Gmail**:
    o   Go to **Gmail** and log in to your account.
2. **Step 2: Compose a New Email**:
    o   Click on the **Compose** button to start a new email.
3. **Step 3: Attach Files from Google Drive**:
    o   In the email composition window, click on the **Google Drive icon** (shaped like a triangle) at the bottom of the email.

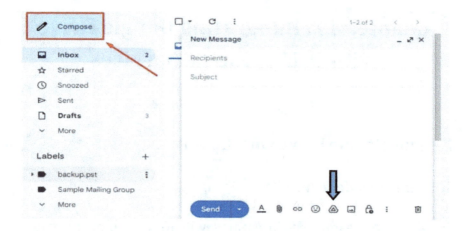

- o This will open a window showing your **Google Drive files**.

4. **Step 4: Select Files**:
    - o Browse through your Drive and select the file or folder you want to attach. You can use the search bar to quickly locate specific files.
    - o Once selected, click **Insert** to attach the file to the email.

5. **Step 5: Send the Email**:
    - o Finish composing your email and click **Send**. Your recipient will receive a link to access the file in your Google Drive.

Sending Google Drive Links in Gmail

If you don't want to attach a file directly, you can send a **Google Drive link** instead. Here's how to do it:

1. **Step 1: Get the Shareable Link**:
    - o Right-click on the file or folder in **Google Drive** and select **Get link**.

- Adjust the sharing settings (Viewer, Editor, Commenter) depending on how you want the recipient to access the file.
- Click **Copy link**.

2. **Step 2: Paste the Link in Gmail**:
   - Open **Gmail** and start composing your email.
   - Paste the copied link into the body of the email.

3. **Step 3: Send the Email**:
   - Complete the email and send it. The recipient will be able to click on the link and access the shared file or folder from your Google Drive.

2. Integrating Google Drive with Google Photos

Uploading Photos and Videos to Google Drive

You can upload your photos and videos from Google Photos to Google Drive for better storage and access. Here's how you can upload files from Google Photos to Google Drive:

1. **Step 1: Open Google Photos**:
   - Go to the **Google Photos** app or website at photos.google.com.

2. **Step 2: Select Photos or Videos**:
   - Browse your photos and videos and select the ones you want to upload to Google Drive.
   - To select multiple items, click the **checkbox** on each item.

3. **Step 3: Download to Your Device**:

- If you're using a computer, you can download the selected photos or videos to your device by clicking the **three dots menu** and selecting **Download**.
- On mobile, tap **Download** after selecting the items.

4. **Step 4: Upload to Google Drive**:
   - After downloading, open **Google Drive** and navigate to the folder where you want to upload the photos or videos.
   - Click the **+ (plus sign)** in the lower-right corner, then select **Upload** and choose the files you just downloaded from Google Photos.

Accessing and Managing Google Photos within Drive

Google Drive automatically shows a **Google Photos folder** if you have connected your Google Photos account to Drive. Here's how to access and manage photos:

1. **Step 1: Open Google Drive**:
   - Go to **Google Drive** at drive.google.com and sign in.
2. **Step 2: Find the Google Photos Folder**:
   - In the left sidebar, look for a folder named **Google Photos**.
   - Click to open it and see your synced photos.
3. **Step 3: Organize and Manage Files**:
   - You can organize photos by moving them into specific folders within Google Drive.
   - You can also delete or share photos directly from this folder.
4. **Step 4: Sharing Google Photos from Drive**:

o   Right-click on any photo in the Google Photos folder and select **Share** to send the photo via link or email.

3. Google Drive and Google Keep Integration

Using Google Keep with Google Drive

Google Keep is a note-taking app that integrates seamlessly with Google Drive, allowing you to store and manage your notes alongside your files. Here's how you can use Google Keep within Google Drive:

1. **Step 1: Open Google Keep**:
   o   Go to **Google Keep** at keep.google.com and sign in with your Google account.
2. **Step 2: Create a Note**:
   o   Click on the **Take a note** field and start typing your note. You can add text, checkboxes, and even voice memos.
3. **Step 3: Link Keep Notes to Google Drive**:
   o   In the note, click on the **three dots menu** and select **Add to Google Drive**.
   o   The note will now be linked to your Google Drive, and you can access it directly from the **Google Drive** web interface.

Adding Notes to Your Google Drive Files

You can also attach Google Keep notes to specific files stored in Google Drive. Here's how:

1. **Step 1: Open a Google Drive File**:

   o Open a Google Docs, Sheets, or Slides file in Google Drive.

2. **Step 2: Open Google Keep Sidebar**:
   o In the file, click on **Tools** in the top menu and select **Keep notepad** to open the Keep sidebar.

3. **Step 3: Add a Note**:
   o From the sidebar, click **Take a note** to create a new note or select an existing note from the list to attach it to the document.

4. **Step 4: Access the Note**:
   o Your note will appear alongside your file in the sidebar, and you can easily reference it while working on your document.

Chapter 12: Using Google Drive for Collaboration in Teams

1. Google Drive Team Drives

Setting Up and Using Team Drives

Google Drive's **Team Drives** (now called **Shared Drives**) allow teams to collaborate on files and documents in a shared space. This feature is ideal for businesses, educational institutions, or any group working together on projects. Here's how to set up and use **Shared Drives**:

1. **Step 1: Access Google Drive**:
    o   Go to **Google Drive** at drive.google.com and sign in to your account.
2. **Step 2: Create a Shared Drive**:
    o   On the left-hand sidebar, click on **Shared Drives**.
    o   Click the **+ (plus sign)** at the top left of the page to create a new Shared Drive.
    o   Enter a name for your Shared Drive (e.g., "Marketing Team" or "Project X").

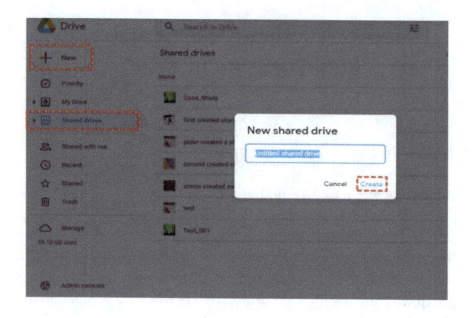

3. **Step 3: Add Files to the Shared Drive**:
    o Open the Shared Drive you just created.
    o You can now add files by clicking the **+ (plus sign)** or dragging files from your computer into the drive.
4. **Step 4: Organize Files in Folders**:
    o To keep your files organized, create folders within the Shared Drive by clicking on the **+ New Folder** option. You can arrange files by type or project.

Managing Team Drive Permissions and Members

Managing access to a **Shared Drive** is critical for ensuring that only the right people can view or edit files. Here's how to manage permissions and members:

1. **Step 1: Open Shared Drive Settings**:

- In your **Shared Drive**, click the **three dots menu** (More options) next to the drive name.
- Select **Manage Members** to view and adjust member permissions.

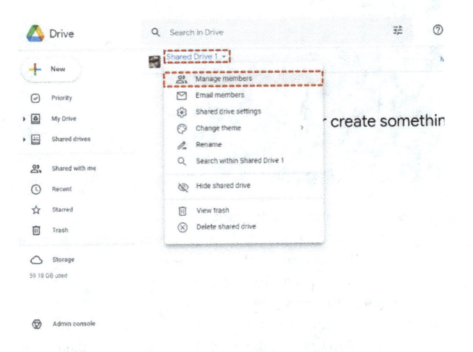

2. **Step 2: Adding Members**:
   - In the Manage Members window, enter the email addresses of people you want to add.
   - Choose the level of access for each person: **Manager**, **Content Manager**, **Contributor**, **Commenter**, or **Viewer**.
   - Click **Send Invitation** to add them to the drive.

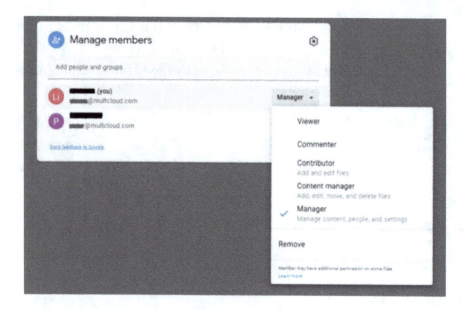

3. **Step 3: Adjust Permissions**:
   - To change permissions, go to **Manage Members**, find the user, and click the drop-down next to their name. Select the desired permission level.
4. **Step 4: Removing Members**:
   - To remove someone from the Shared Drive, go to **Manage Members**, click the **X** next to their name, and confirm their removal.

2. Collaborating with Google Workspace

Integrating Google Drive with Google Docs, Sheets, Slides, and Meet for Teams

Google Workspace (formerly G Suite) integrates seamlessly with **Google Drive**, offering powerful tools for collaboration. Here's how you can integrate **Docs**, **Sheets**, **Slides**, and **Meet** for efficient team collaboration:

1. **Step 1: Google Docs for Team Collaboration**:
    - Open **Google Docs** from Google Drive by clicking **+ New** and selecting **Google Docs**.

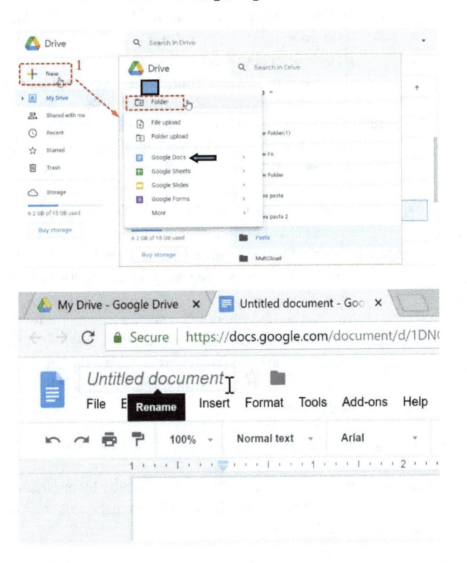

- Once the document is created, you can invite collaborators by clicking the **Share** button at the top right.
- Add people by email and choose their permission levels (Viewer, Commenter, Editor).

2. **Step 2: Google Sheets for Collaborative Spreadsheets**:
   - In **Google Sheets**, you can work on real-time data with your team. Click **+ New** in Drive, then select **Google Sheets** to create a spreadsheet.
   - Use features like **comments** and **suggestions** to track changes and collaborate effectively.

3. **Step 3: Google Slides for Collaborative Presentations**:
   - Create presentations in **Google Slides** by selecting **Google Slides** under the **+ New** button in Drive.
   - Share the presentation with team members and work together in real-time. You can edit, comment, and suggest changes simultaneously.

4. **Step 4: Google Meet for Video Conferencing**:
   - Google Meet allows seamless video meetings with team members.
   - You can easily schedule or start a meeting directly from Google Calendar, with the meeting link included. Once the meeting is created, you can share the link in the **Google Docs**, **Sheets**, or **Slides** files for easy access.

Organizing Group Projects and Collaborating on Files

Google Drive allows teams to collaborate efficiently by organizing group projects and sharing files. Here's how to make the most of Drive for project collaboration:

1. **Step 1: Create Project Folders**:
   - In **Google Drive**, create a folder specifically for your group project (e.g., "Project X Documents").
   - Organize this folder with subfolders for different tasks, such as **Research**, **Budget**, or **Marketing Materials**.
2. **Step 2: Share Files and Folders**:
   - Share the folder with your team by right-clicking on it and selecting **Share**.
   - You can grant different permissions for different team members, ensuring that only authorized individuals can edit specific documents.
3. **Step 3: Collaborate Using Comments and Suggestions**:
   - **Google Docs**, **Sheets**, and **Slides** allow you to add comments, making collaboration easier.
   - Highlight text or data and click the **Comment** button to add feedback or questions.
   - You can also **suggest edits** instead of making permanent changes, giving others the opportunity to approve or decline suggestions.
4. **Step 4: Track Changes with Version History**:
   - All Google Drive files have version history. To access it, click **File > Version history > See version history**. You can view previous versions and revert to an earlier one if necessary.
   - This is especially useful for group projects where multiple team members are working on the same document simultaneously.
5. **Step 5: Real-Time Collaboration**:

- Google Drive's real-time collaboration features allow everyone on your team to work together at the same time.
- You'll see who is online and can see their changes live as they type, making it easier to collaborate without the need for back-and-forth emails.

Chapter 13: Troubleshooting Google Drive

1. Fixing Common Google Drive Errors

Resolving Syncing Issues

Syncing issues can prevent your files from being updated across devices, leading to inconsistent file versions. Here's how to troubleshoot syncing issues in Google Drive:

1. **Check Your Internet Connection**:
   - A weak or intermittent connection can cause syncing issues. Ensure you have a stable internet connection.
2. **Ensure Google Drive is Running**:
   - On your desktop, check if the **Google Drive Backup and Sync** or **Drive for Desktop** application is running.
   - On mobile, make sure the Google Drive app is up to date and running.
3. **Pause and Resume Syncing**:
   - Right-click the Google Drive icon on your desktop and select **Pause syncing**. After a few seconds, click **Resume syncing** to restart the sync process.
4. **Check for Updates**:
   - Ensure you are using the latest version of the Google Drive app or software. Outdated versions may cause

syncing issues. Update the app from the **Google Play Store** (for Android) or **App Store** (for iOS).

5. **Reinstall Google Drive**:
   o If syncing issues persist, try uninstalling and reinstalling Google Drive on both desktop and mobile devices to reset the sync process.

Fixing Upload and Download Problems

If you encounter problems while uploading or downloading files, follow these troubleshooting steps:

1. **Check Your Storage**:
   o Ensure you have enough space in your Google Drive account. If your storage is full, you won't be able to upload more files.
   o Check your available storage under **Settings** in Google Drive, and if necessary, delete unnecessary files or upgrade your storage plan.
2. **File Size and Type Limitations**:
   o Ensure that the files you're uploading aren't exceeding Google Drive's file size limit (15GB for individual files).
   o Also, check that your file format is supported by Google Drive.
3. **Clear Browser Cache and Cookies**:
   o If you're using the web version of Google Drive, clearing your browser's cache and cookies can resolve issues related to uploading or downloading files.
4. **Use Incognito Mode**:

- o Sometimes, browser extensions can interfere with uploads or downloads. Try using **Incognito Mode** in your browser to see if the issue persists.
5. **Try a Different Browser or Device**:
   - o If the issue is with the browser, try uploading or downloading using a different browser, such as Chrome, Firefox, or Safari, or try another device to see if the problem is specific to your setup.

Error Messages in Google Drive and How to Solve Them

Google Drive may display error messages when something goes wrong. Below are common errors and their solutions:

1. **Error 404: File Not Found**:
   - o This error occurs if you try to access a file that has been deleted or moved to another location.
   - o Solution: Double-check the file location or check your **Trash** for deleted files.
2. **Error 500: Internal Server Error**:
   - o This error happens when Google Drive encounters server issues.
   - o Solution: Wait a few minutes and try again. If the issue persists, check Google's **G Suite Status Dashboard** for updates.
3. **"Quota Exceeded" Error**:
   - o This error occurs when you've used all your available storage space.
   - o Solution: Free up space by deleting unnecessary files or upgrade to a higher Google One storage plan.
4. **"File Is Too Large" Error**:

- o This error happens if your file exceeds the allowed size for Google Drive.
- o Solution: Reduce the file size or use a different service for larger files, such as Google Photos or Google Video.

2. Google Drive App Issues on Mobile

Solving Syncing and Upload Issues on Mobile Devices

Mobile syncing issues can prevent you from accessing or uploading files on your smartphone or tablet. To resolve these issues:

1. **Check Your Internet Connection**:
   - o A slow or unstable connection can hinder syncing. Ensure you have a reliable Wi-Fi or mobile data connection.
2. **Update the Google Drive App**:
   - o Outdated apps may cause syncing issues. Go to the **Google Play Store** or **Apple App Store** and ensure that you have the latest version of the Google Drive app.
3. **Enable Background Data**:
   - o If syncing isn't happening in the background, go to your device's settings and ensure that **Background App Refresh** (iOS) or **Background Data** (Android) is enabled for Google Drive.
4. **Manually Sync Files**:
   - o Open the Google Drive app and tap on the file you want to sync. If it's not syncing automatically, try

manually refreshing by pulling down the screen to force a sync.

5. **Re-login to Google Account**:
   - o   If syncing problems persist, sign out and sign back into your Google account on the Google Drive app. This may reset any temporary issues with syncing.

Clearing Cache and Data for Google Drive App

If the Google Drive app is still experiencing issues like sync errors or crashes, clearing the app's cache or data may resolve the problem:

1. **Clear Cache (Android)**:
   - o   Open **Settings** on your device.
   - o   Go to **Apps** or **Application Manager** and select **Google Drive**.
   - o   Tap **Storage**, then tap **Clear Cache**.
2. **Clear Data (Android)**:
   - o   In the same storage menu, tap **Clear Data** to reset the app. Keep in mind that this will log you out and remove any locally stored files, but it will not delete files in Google Drive.
3. **Clear Cache and Reinstall (iOS)**:
   - o   iOS doesn't have a cache clearing option, so you may need to delete the app and reinstall it. After reinstalling, sign back into your Google account.
4. **Check App Permissions**:
   - o   Make sure that Google Drive has the necessary permissions to access storage and sync files. Go to

Settings > Apps > Google Drive and enable permissions for **Storage** and **Network Access**.

Chapter 14: Advanced Google Drive Features

1. Automating Tasks with Google Apps Script

Introduction to Google Apps Script

Google Apps Script is a powerful tool that allows you to automate tasks and integrate Google Drive with other Google services. It's a scripting platform built into Google Drive that uses JavaScript to create custom workflows. You can automate repetitive tasks, streamline processes, and enhance productivity within your Google Drive.

Key Benefits:

- Create custom functions to automate tasks.
- Automate email notifications for file changes or uploads.
- Automatically move or rename files based on certain conditions.

How to Automate File Organization and Management

Google Apps Script can help organize your files by automating the process of sorting and managing your documents in Google Drive. Here's a basic overview of what you can do:

1. **Creating Scripts to Organize Files**:

- You can write a script to automatically move files to different folders based on their names, types, or other conditions.
- Example: Move all files with the word "Report" in their title to a folder named "Reports."

Sample Script:

```
function moveReports() {
 var folder = DriveApp.getFolderById('your-folder-id'); // Folder to move files to
 var files = DriveApp.getFilesByName('Report'); // Files with "Report" in their name
 while (files.hasNext()) {
  var file = files.next();
  folder.createFile(file); // Moves the file to the designated folder
 }
}
```

2. **Setting Up Automated Backups:**
   - Use Google Apps Script to create a backup system. For instance, you can automatically copy files from one folder to another every night.

Example Script for Daily Backups:

```
function backupFiles() {
 var sourceFolder = DriveApp.getFolderById('source-folder-id');
```

```
var targetFolder = DriveApp.getFolderById('backup-folder-id');
 var files = sourceFolder.getFiles();
 while (files.hasNext()) {
  var file = files.next();
  targetFolder.createFile(file); // Copies file to backup folder
 }
}
```

3. **Automating File Renaming**:
   o Rename files based on specific patterns, such as adding dates or changing file extensions. For instance, you could rename files to include the current date.

Example Script for Renaming Files:

CopyEdit
```
function renameFiles() {
 var folder = DriveApp.getFolderById('your-folder-id');
 var files = folder.getFiles();
 var date = new Date();
 while (files.hasNext()) {
  var file = files.next();
  var newName = file.getName() + "_" + date.toISOString();
  file.setName(newName);
 }
}
```

Setting Up Google Apps Script

To set up Google Apps Script:

1. Open **Google Drive**.
2. Click on the **New** button, go to **More**, and select **Google Apps Script**.
3. Create your script in the script editor.
4. Save and run the script as needed. You can also set up triggers to automate tasks at regular intervals (e.g., daily backups).

2. Integrating Third-Party Apps with Google Drive

Using Zapier with Google Drive

Zapier is an online automation tool that connects your favorite apps and services, enabling them to work together without any manual effort. By integrating Google Drive with Zapier, you can automate workflows between Google Drive and hundreds of other apps.

1. **Setting Up a Zap**:
   - **Create a Zap**: In Zapier, you can create "Zaps," which are automated workflows that connect Google Drive to other apps.
   - **Choose a Trigger**: For example, you could set Google Drive as the trigger. A common trigger might be "New File in Folder."
   - **Choose an Action**: For example, after a new file is uploaded, you might want to send a notification via Slack, add a task in Trello, or save the file to Dropbox.

Example Use Case:

- Trigger: A new file is uploaded to a specific Google Drive folder.
- Action: The file is automatically added to a task management app like **Trello** or **Asana**.

2. **Popular Google Drive Zapier Integrations**:
   - **Google Drive + Gmail**: Automatically email files from Google Drive when they are uploaded to a folder.
   - **Google Drive + Slack**: Send notifications in Slack whenever new files are added to Google Drive.
   - **Google Drive + Dropbox**: Automatically copy files between Google Drive and Dropbox.
   - **Google Drive + Google Sheets**: Automatically log new file names and details into a Google Sheets spreadsheet.

How to Set Up a Google Drive Zap

1. Sign up for a **Zapier** account.
2. Click **Make a Zap**.
3. For the **Trigger** app, search for **Google Drive** and choose a trigger (e.g., "New File in Folder").
4. Connect your Google Drive account and set up the trigger conditions (e.g., select the folder).
5. For the **Action** app, search for and choose the app you want to integrate with Google Drive (e.g., Gmail, Slack, etc.).
6. Set up the action conditions and map data (e.g., send an email with the file attachment).
7. Test the Zap and turn it on.

Connecting Google Drive to Other Productivity Apps

You can connect Google Drive to other productivity apps to streamline your workflow. Here are a few examples of integrations that enhance productivity:

1. **Trello + Google Drive**:
   - Attach Google Drive files directly to Trello cards. When a file is updated in Drive, the changes will reflect in the Trello card.
2. **Asana + Google Drive**:
   - Add Google Drive files to tasks in Asana for easier collaboration. Attach files from Google Drive to specific projects or tasks.
3. **Evernote + Google Drive**:
   - Store Google Drive files directly in Evernote, or create a note that includes a link to a file stored in Google Drive.
4. **Slack + Google Drive**:
   - Share Google Drive files directly in Slack channels. This integration is useful for team collaboration, making it easy to share documents and get feedback in real-time.
5. **Google Drive + Microsoft Office**:
   - With Zapier or other integrations, you can use Microsoft Office files (Word, Excel, PowerPoint) alongside your Google Drive files, making collaboration easier for teams using different tools.

Index

www.ingramcontent.com/pod-product-compliance
Lightning Source LLC
La Vergne TN
LVHW012335060326
832902LV00012B/1903